AF362329

Poems On Corporate Life

A collection on how office life looks like

Nikita Sood

BookLeaf Publishing

India | USA | UK

Copyright © Nikita Sood
All Rights Reserved.

This book has been self-published with all reasonable efforts taken to make the material error-free by the author. No part of this book shall be used, reproduced in any manner whatsoever without written permission from the author, except in the case of brief quotations embodied in critical articles and reviews.

The Author of this book is solely responsible and liable for its content including but not limited to the views, representations, descriptions, statements, information, opinions, and references ["Content"]. The Content of this book shall not constitute or be construed or deemed to reflect the opinion or expression of the Publisher or Editor. Neither the Publisher nor Editor endorse or approve the Content of this book or guarantee the reliability, accuracy, or completeness of the Content published herein and do not make any representations or warranties of any kind, express or implied, including but not limited to the implied warranties of merchantability, fitness for a particular purpose.

The Publisher and Editor shall not be liable whatsoever...

Made with ❤ on the BookLeaf Publishing Platform
www.bookleafpub.in
www.bookleafpub.com

Dedication

Dedicated to all my avid readers

Preface

"Poems on Corporate Life: A collection on how office life looks like" is created out of the experiences of corporate employees. These poems are a reflection on how a corporate employee journeys through his career, from facing the interview panel, getting onboarded, dealing with a robust manager, owning up to the work, responsibilities that come with promotion, so on and so forth.

Having more than 10 years of experience in the corporate world, I was rest assured of sharing experiences. As you delve into these poems, you will find a very real relatability aspect.

Acknowledgements

Family life is a life full of responsibilities.

My heartfelt gratitude to all family members for sharing responsibilities to help me find time to finish this work of writing, I had always wanted to accomplish. I truly understand the importance of the support of family to realize one's goals in life.

THE HR ROUND OF JOB INTERVIEW

Her efforts rippled through the quiet,
She struggled to get that job, as she worked untired.

As she made her way to the interview room,
Poised to live a life of toil, she chimed in, that she was
ready to bloom.

The panel was apprehensive of her capabilities,
Round 2 was scheduled to further examine her skills and
abilities.

Depressed over her doubtful selection,
She kept her focus without any deviation.

Her career was on a knife's edge,
The requirements of this round, were higher, for the
bench.

The deciding round came to an end, and her anxiety

grew,

The HR said, "WE WILL GET BACK TO YOU"!

INTRODUCTION WITH THE MD, A HEARTFELT MEETING

After almost a week of joining the Company,
We received a heartwarming welcome from the founder,
so warm and homely.

He emphasized on the core principles, the values and the
vision,
Commitment to serve with excellence and ethics, laying
down a strong foundation.

Extending gratitude towards the efforts of employees
and support members,
His tribute to the company's stakeholders, that he
always remembers.

He heard a few of us, expressing thankfulness,
An opportunity to work for the Company, with vigour
and truthfulness.

The closing note came with best wishes for a bright
future,
A meeting, the new joiners will always treasure.

THE ERROR

The error that gave me sleepless nights,
The debit entries were wrongly entered as credit, in
broad daylights.

Until the supervisor was unaware of the mistake,
I was petrified of getting an earful, for giving an
explanation so vague.

The next day, I took half a day off, to save face,
The supervisor now, not unaware, asked me to redo each
and every case.

This time, the supervisor's eyes were on me,
Making sure I did not go on breaks or take a leave.

Finally, I managed to clear every discrepancy,
Finishing the rework impeccably.

Although the supervisor did not fail to take cognizance

of my mistake,
Thankfully, my position in the Company was still safe!

WHO WILL DO YOUR WORK WHEN YOU ARE AWAY?

She wanted to get her planned leaves approved,
She was too intimidated by her robust manager, so loud
and rude.

The manager said ''Who will do your work when you are
away''?
The most loyal team-mate stepped up "I will come in
handy when she is on holiday".

"Punctuality is the cornerstone of the upcoming project
", argued the boss,
The team came to the forefront of the situation, "We will
cover up for her, ensuring there is no loss".

Unity rose above physical limitation,
Changing the manager's stern perception.

THE PROBLEM SOLVER SUPERVISOR

The supervisor possessed extraordinary problem-solving ability,
She tackled challenges with innovative solutions and so much agility.

Her ideas never failed to amaze,
Her answers were precise always.

Even in the most pressing situations,
She had resourceful and simple solutions.

Her practical approach to circumstances,
Made it easy to face difficulties.

Her way of working gained recognition,
Her brilliance was admired and received adulation.

ANNUAL INCREMENTS

The highly anticipated annual increments were just
announced,
The enthusiastic employees showed mixed emotions, a
few were happy, but some still had doubts.

The decision was taken behind closed doors,
The transparency was questioned, raising eyebrows.

The HR said it is a matter of confidentiality,
The employees questioned its rationality.

The employees resisted, showing discontent,
The company defended, 'claiming sensitive information
to be kept a secret.'

THE STALWART

With 20 years in the industry, she is a stalwart,
She has been pushing boundaries to make her mark.

Exploring roles and opportunities,
She was quick to step up into training and development
activities.

With a low start in this new venture,
She picked up the pace to meet the demands of sessions
and all the lectures.

Leading from the front, her sessions gained popularity
far and wide,
The stalwart's success was no surprise; she was already
poised for her impending promotion with all the pride.

OVERWORKING AS A SELF LESS BEING

He knew it was time to say 'no',
But his self-less nature, made him not to let go.

He is the team's spearhead,
Always delivers with effortless fineness.

With herculean efforts, he made a mark,
But one man cannot replace a team's job, with how
much so ever spark.

Better team players were the need of the hour,
Relying heavily on him even with so much manpower.

He never calculated his statistical overtime,
Selflessly thriving each day, never bothering about being
in the limelight.

PROMOTION, A GOOD OR BAD CHOICE

He was the star performer of the team,
Spearheading software testing in all its means.

From an experienced teammate to a full-time team leader,
A decision taken by the board, readily agreed to by the uncompromising seeker.

Acknowledging his performance, he was rewarded with the promotion,
But the added responsibilities, deterred him from keeping his focus, even though he worked with so much devotion.

The manager argued, a great performer does not always make for a good leader,
Being carried away, losing specialists skillset, destroying a promising career.

THE PROJECT'S TEAM SELECTION

Fresh faces were given priority,
The selection emphasised versatility.

The last projects' stellar performers also stood in the
race,
The experienced associates were also given a place.

The retired paved way for the new entrants,
Leaving no feeling of repentance.

A senior official took a leave of absence,
Next in the hierarchy, took charge of maintaining a
balance.

The squad comprised of the young and the experienced,
To keep a constant check on law and surveillance.

STAR WITHOUT HARDSHIPS

Awarding the star performer of the week,
A common practice for employee motivation indeed.

The team member with minimum discrepancies to his
name,
Will be called as the star, the supervisor proclaimed.

She outdid all other associates of the team,
She was pronounced, star performer for the week.

A few eyebrows were raised,
Questioning her bandwidth, despite all the praise.

A star without the hardships
Responsibility sharing, it was time to upgrade skills.

THE EXTENDED WORK HOURS

Being reserved was mostly my way.
But that day, was an unusual day,

I was wearing my heart on my sleeve,
I expressed disagreement openly, on unsustainable
working hours for more than a week.

The entire week, we worked way beyond the stipulated
office timings,
To avoid piling up any kind of pendencies.

The requirements of the project were high,
We worked late to meet the project's demands, without
any upside.

The manager lent us an ear,
Though, there were still no perks, he managed to limit
the work, crafting a system so clear.

ARE YOU BOSS'S FAVOURITE

It is not about being faithful towards leadership,
It is about showing integrity and commitment towards
the organization's partnership.

The idea is not flattering top leaders' psychologies,
The real work is strengthening the entity's ideologies.

Showing dissent is not disloyalty,
It is a rather robust step towards developing a genuine
ideology.

It is not about working in accord with the demands of
the manager,
It has more to do with serving the needs of the
organization's order.

Developing a culture that values integrity,
Over a system that supports unnecessary adulatory.

THE REPORT

All eyes were set on the weekly report,
Presented by the finance department to all the teams and
the panel on board.

The report reviews the company's financial health over
the last week,
It provides insights into the company's receivables,
outstanding bills, and overdue payments which are at
their peak.

This report is an understanding of the company's
payments and receivables trends,
It is closely followed by the customer and payments
team, also keeping a check on borrowings and spends.

The report helps in planning for the coming week's
financial position,
Giving a glimpse of a few financial indicators, in line
with the company's mission.

HIGH COMPLEXITY PROJECT

The success of the high-complexity project,
Is a story in itself so clean and perfect.

It is attributed to the hard work of the debutants,
The power and influence of the experienced.

The passion and dedication of raw and fresh talent,
Exploring avenues, eager to learn, fearless and gallant.

The veterans were navigating the complexities,
Anticipating the difficulties and uncertainties.

The success of the project is tickling the company's bank
books,
The debutants are hopeful of a promising future,
veterans of easing their bill books.

THE WORKAHOLIC

Employees show up to make a living,
They work to earn money, for future savings.

Most of them work for personal goals,
However, some of them, care about the outcome of their
work on the whole.

A few of them are deeply invested in their role,
They perform their duties without attachment to the
personal result, giving their heart and soul.

Right intentions and maintaining integrity,
Knowing the higher purpose and the greater mission,
also helps in achieving prosperity.

TRUST IN THE TEAM LEAD

The position of the team lead was insecure,
The relationship with the team members was unstable,
which had no cure.

He was the mainstay of the project,
To part ways with him, was not an idea so perfect.

He was seen as a more outspoken individual,
Who failed to gain the trust of the team, despite being
highly intellectual.

If the project fails to deliver noticeably,
His wings will be clipped unarguably.

Accountability failure, lack of trust in the team,
All eyes were on him, to end the regime.

THAT FEELING OF BEING LEFT OUT OR DROPPED OUT

It was a project of high value,
In all, they needed 10 people, who could break through.

Fingers were crossed for the rare opportunity,
Everyone desperately wanted to be a part of the project
so revolutionary.

A feeling of turmoil took over,
Baffled by the announcement of the promoter.

Although, the decision raised a few eyebrows,
It led to the thought, time has already caught up, to
announce retirement vows.

KINDNESS IS SELF REWARDING

A team member was piled up with pendency,
Leaving work for tomorrow, was his tendency.

The manager refused to extend the deadline beyond this
day,
The associate was completely wound up, looking at me
in dismay.

Already 4.5 hours of overtime,
I helped him in achieving the task, within the stipulated
time.

Even though it was not my role,
I helped him, leaving behind my priorities at home.

There was no external recognition or reward for my
kindness,

It was inherently self-rewarding, for my own happiness
and internal wellness.

SERVING THE NOTICE

After 15 years of relentless service,
He decided to call it a day and serve the notice.

With heart and mind in sync, he made a clear decision,
It was time to move on, to take up a new position.

Wearing an overwhelming and emotional look,
He broke the news to his manager, who was busy
reading the bank book.

The manager was taken by surprise,
But accepted his decision, which was so wise.

His prowess as a leader was indeed admired,
The stellar leaving behind a legacy, so much inspired.

THE BEST COMPLIMENT

After 10 years of my stint in the Company,
Colleagues had to say a few goodbye words, not so
casually.

A teammate said, the best leader, I worked with,
Another said, meeting deadlines, even without
bandwidth.

Someone said, they admired me for my brilliance,
While some liked my patience, a few adored my
resilience.

Compliments were way too many as a proud employee,
But the best one, which my family upheld, I did fairly
well in my life!

www.ingramcontent.com/pod-product-compliance
Lightning Source LLC
LaVergne TN
LVHW010952200726

843509LV00013B/2376